Every Sunset is a Moonrise

Faith, Poetry, Finitude

Matthew A. Stanley

SAMSARA
DIAGNOSTICS

Samsara Diagnostics

Contents

Chapter One

Introduction

Introductory remarks

The art of *waka* poetry was said to have originated when the brother of the Sun goddess Amaterasu had completed building a house for his bride, intoning these words[1] :

> Here, where eight clouds rise
> In the land of Izumo
> I will house my beloved
> Inside an eightfold fence
> Inside an eightfold fence

---

1. Makoto Ueda. *Modern Japanese Tanka*. (New York: Columbia University Press, 1996), x.

One who composes using the *waka* form employs only thirty-one syllables, typically divided into five lines of 5-7-5-7-7. The style lends itself to short and elegant observations concerning life, nature, and one's own heart. This brief form of poetry dominated the Japanese poetic arts from early on, composing 4,200 of the 4,500 poems in the earliest official collection of Japanese poetry, the *Manyoshu*, dating to the mid 8th century AD.[2]

I first encountered Saigyo, a poet-monk and one of the great *waka* masters from the 12th century, when I read his work in a Japanese literature class in college. He inspired me to attempt composing my own thoughts in the *waka* form. As someone particularly given to speculative and analytical work, *waka* struck me as an opportunity to challenge myself to capture the essence of an experience whilst using few words. Later in this book, you will find the collection which I produced, followed by some brief interpretations of select poems. I share this all with you under the same title as this book — *Every Sunset is a Moonrise.*

***

I've chosen this title for two primary reasons —

First, I composed this work for my undergraduate senior capstone seminar which focused on the question "what is the good life?" As I first read Saigyo's poetry in a class I was taking that semester, I began

---

2. Ibid., xi.

to see both the life of Saigyo and the practice of composing *waka* as two unexpected resources for exploring the nature of the good life.

It was the end of 2017, and in less than 8 months I would be finishing college, so I was turning my attention with renewed urgency to what my next steps would look like. In particular, I was grappling with the question of whether to continue pursuing my dream of becoming a professor of philosophy. Should I apply to graduate programs, or find a different path? And if so, which one? In light of that personal struggle, I found it particularly fitting to consider how the end of that season in my life simultaneously composed a new beginning.

Serendipitously, at the same time that I was reading Saigyo and writing *waka*, I was also in a philosophy seminar where we were reading Heidegger's *Being and Time*. In the philosophical movement called Phenomenology, of which Heidegger was a foremost thinker, practitioners pay close attention to the details of particular experiences, observing their reactions, mental states, and the variations of the object in their field of perception.

As I learned to practice Husserl's phenomenological method for myself, and read Heidegger's analysis of human existence through the lens of time and death, I began to see how *waka* could function as a phenomenology of finitude. *Waka* awakened me to notice the beauty of things passing away and the essentially indeterminate process of becoming, both of which impressed themselves upon me as vital components of any theory of knowledge which takes finitude seriously as a condition of human experience.

Thus, secondly, I came to see how a sunset also constituting a moonrise captures the way that one must look at phenomena when composing *waka* — the dual aspect of all things. Every experience includes both a being-born and a passing-away, united by our experience of a singular moment of becoming. This multivalence inherent to every experience drives the journey of finite creatures as we discover our world and the others we find alongside ourselves in that world. In the end, *waka* became for me a noticing and rejoicing in being a creature who finds their flourishing *through* limits, rather than attempting to cast them off.

Exploring the contours of finitude

In Christian traditions of philosophical and theological inquiry, the notion of finitude has typically been developed through a process of negation with respect to some theory about the infinite nature of God. If God is entirely self-existent, He cannot be dependent upon those things which He created, but rather they must be wholly other from and dependent upon Him. As the ground of Being, He is also beyond Being. In like manner, many theologians proceed to derive a number of attributes about God, and concurrently, about *us* who are the created. We are utterly unlike God, and this radical otherness from God constitutes the essence of our finitude as creatures.

This much is true — we are not God and God is not like us in many crucial respects. Nonetheless, we can also build a generative account of finitude which takes our limitations precisely as its starting point, and not as deviations from the impossible shape of eternity. By shifting our perspective, we can see that our un-likeness to God also provides us the parameters within which we operate as creatures, and this fresh vision can motivate a properly humble and curious bottom-up investigation of creaturely life.

We might interpret the project of Western philosophy after Descartes as an attempt to enunciate the elementary generative structures which produce our experience as finite beings. As Kant observes, our experience must take place within the parameters of time and space. No experience outside these two coordinates can be expressed or represented (although the door remains open that such a thing could, nonetheless, still be an experience). Some of the other structures which philosophers have enunciated as necessary for consciousness include phenomena such as bodies, language, absence, and even other persons.

Thus, while many have chosen to focus on how finitude falls short of infinity, we may just as easily say that finitude's testimony to the radical otherness of the Creator simultaneously attests to the unique constitution of the otherness of the creature as well, and thus issues a call to re-immerse ourselves in the adventure of finitude once more.

It was Jamie Smith's *Desiring the Kingdom* which first woke me up to the need for a theological inquiry which was sufficiently curious about the actual structure and operation of finite creatures. Rather than deciding ahead of time how things *should* be or espousing a fixed abstract system ("worldview"), we would be far better served by careful and courageous observation of the world which God made, including human minds and behavior. Smith's book contributes to this endeavor by calling into question the operative theory in evangelical theology which sees right beliefs as the primary motivator for right action — what if, Smith asks, exactly the opposite is true? What if love guides and norms our beliefs, and what if it's precisely our actions which shape what we love in the first place?

Smith's work provided an early model for me as a budding theologian, and his text *The Fall of Interpretation* brought many pieces together for me as a Christian philosopher. In his questioning of the predominant evangelical paradigms in which I had been raised, I began to glimpse the possibilities of a finitude which testifies both to its otherness *and* to its *goodness.* The limits and structures of creaturely life began to emerge not as chains to be thrown off or dangerous lies to be disproven, but rather as pregnant phenomena which promised a deeper journey into the heart of what God has made, and by extension, into the communion which God has prepared for His creation. If God has made us finite, and thus unlike Himself, then it is right and proper that we be such. Finitude does not encourage us to escape it — it invites us to embrace it as an *adventure*.

We should take this metaphor of adventure seriously. Adventure assumes a narrative of events which are lived by characters which unfold over time, all suffused with the promise of bringing about some new state of affairs. This narrative is experienced from within by the ones living it as a not-yet-knowing-the-outcome, and thus the story only comes to possess a unity *in retrospect*. This is its narratival quality. Life, truth, and meaning all have this narrative structure of anticipation and retrospection.

The narrative proceeds from one point to the next, following a particular path, and it is precisely *this* path and not *that* path. This not-yet-knowing-the-outcome into which those persons within the narrative penetrate has the character of being promissory. It beckons because it contains a new fullness or a higher unity which calls out to us for its own arrival. This as-yet mysterious future represents a possibly which might become actualized, but which is not yet. The path must be followed in time and space in order to bring this possibility into being, whereas following a different path would bring about another possibility entirely. This narrative structures and its path dependency provides the shape of the finite creature's experience of God's world.

With his concept of *Dasein*, Martin Heidegger helps us to see a number of the crucial structures of the adventure we embark on as finite creatures. His Da-sein ("being-there") highlights the there-ness of creaturely life, as opposed to the no-where and every-where of God. Because God is omnipresent, His there is the There of all theres. However, we subsist and find our there within His every-where and all-encompassing There. We possess a limited there — a specific location — in which we find ourselves. I am sitting *here* writing *these* words. You are *there* reading them. I am not in Tokyo, on the surface of the moon, or down the hall — our there provides the possibility of any here which could be experienced (or loved!).

Our here only appears through relation to a larger there — in this case, a world. We have talked about God's all-encompassing There, but God's There creates the world in which every there can be experienced as a here. A world is not properly the *collection* of objects which by piling up amount to a world, but rather our world serves as the horizon within which objects can become present to us *as objects*. The world derives its function as a limit by representing the totality of significances itself. Our world is overflowing with other things which are both with us and exceed us by virtue of our being-together in this world. These things with us hold out various possible configurations of being-together, both presently and in the future, just like the not-yet-known outcome for the subjects of the adventure.

As we investigate our world and the objects which we share our world with, we begin to discover the limits of our there. We only find a specific set of objects there with us in our world. Just as we are finite, those objects which we can be with in our there are necessarily finite too. This constitutes our "thrown-ness," in Heidegger's words. The image of being thrown evokes the sense of having found ourselves to be somewhere *already*. There is a thrower and the one thrown[3], and this primordially past event of being thrown underlies my experience of having a world and set of possibilities. For instance, I didn't choose to be born, much less to whom, when, or where. I entered the history of this world *in media res*, and I come to find that the point at which I entered this life determined for me those things which could become possibilities, as well as those things which could never be possibilities.

While my thrown-ness certainly limits my possibilities, this fact about my being also has the double aspect of constituting the possibility of my having possibilities. Since I am finite, and thus cannot possess an infinite set of possibilities, my having come to possess a finite set allows me to have possibilities at all. These possibilities are suited to my constitution as a finite being. Because I possess *this* set of possibilities (and not another), these objects, our relations, and our collective possibilities in my world are all I have to work with when it comes to trying to understand myself. They are all I have to make sense of myself with — Nothing more, but also, nothing less. A possibility is a possibility for me in so far as it is something which I can experience and incorporate into what I am. It is a possibility for me to become something else while simultaneously becoming more myself. I can thus become a deeper, fuller me by becoming other-than-me. All of the people, places, and things around me offer this promise of becoming a different and more expansive me through the adventure of finitude.

---

3. Although Heidegger never speaks of a thrower, only ever referring to the experience of "having-been-thrown," the implicit necessity of a *Thrower* is too pregnant to be overlooked.

However, we must realize that this possibility can't simply remain a possibility for me, but it must become a possibility for *us* — me and the other beings together in our world. I am caught up with the things in my world as we are all becoming new and different, both individually and through our constantly evolving relations with each other.

But some of these possibilities for me may be detrimental possibilities or even impossibilities for the objects I am with in my world. This means that I am always in the process of *negotiating* my place within this collective becoming. I have the pleasure and responsibility of being able to partner with other beings in their own journey that they get to actualize as finite creatures, and they get to be a part of my journey as well. Partnering with them allows us to find and actualize new possibilities that we were not aware of before or which could not have been achieved in isolation from each other. Perhaps until I meet a certain person or learned a certain skill, a possibility was not truly mine, but now, because of my becoming party to another being, we are able to discover together a new possibility that neither of us could have imagined.

How does one engage in this negotiation with other beings? This is the task of hermeneutics. Hermeneutics describes the cycle of how finite human beings unfold meaning in the world. As we encounter another object in our world — be it a text, event, animal, or other person — we project possibilities for what we can be together. This initial approach is drawn forward by the invitation of the possibilities this object holds out.

Hermeneutics then involves the corresponding movement of attempting to actualize that possibility, and thereby carrying out some process of assimilation. However, because the object is other, it *resists* this work of integration into my new possibility. The possibility that I have attempted to actualize may not harmonize or agree with that object's possibilities or preferred outcomes. Perhaps it sees things differently than I do. Now we have to go back to the drawing board to adjust and find a new solution.

Hermeneutics demands that we approach again, and we must approach with that humility of spirit which thinks again and proposes another possibility which also includes the objects' projected possibilities, not simply our own. We are being invited into a *dialogue* about what type of world to create together. What will our collective project look like, and how can we get there together? Can we move forward into a future where we actualize something new in our world? What will that something be like? Now we are really on an adventure in time and space.

When we understand the three movement of hermeneutics — projection, resistance, repetition — we see how the uncovering of meaning and consequent actualization of new possibilities necessarily follows an oscillating motion of being in community with others. Thus, we find ourselves in the middle of a grand project of bringing about some complex and interweaving possibility for the world to be. We find that we are playing a specific role in relation to others in precisely the place where we have found ourselves. This movement and mode of play constitutes one of the chief joys of finitude.

Time and death; Arriving and not-Arriving

We have discussed the notion of 'possibility' extensively in the past section, and while this point remained implicit, it has come time to make it explicit — our being-there is inextricably entangled with a that-which-is-not-there. We must speak of "nothingness." The that-which-is-not-there — void, absence, difference — functions in an integral way to our world and everything in it, because nothingness serves as the *ground* of existence.

In Christian theology, nothingness as the ground of existence confronts us in the realization that creation does not possess its life in and of itself — it always derives its life from God who is the effulgent source of all life and existence. Another way of putting this — finite creatures are tenuous and fragile things, always teetering on the edge between existence and non-existence, perpetually liable to fall back into the nothingness from which we emerged.

In the creation narrative as told in the book of Genesis, Yahweh calls creation out of nothingness (*ex nihilo*), which dramatizes how we are quite literally *made of nothing*. The contradiction of being a creature then is that *we are a nothing which has become a something*. Because of this, we are never fully able to leave nothingness behind. It always remains an essential part of our constitution as some-things.

Finitude is marked above all by becoming — an event in which arising and passing away coincide. Becoming presents us with the convergence of both nothing-ness and something-ness. We are not, then we are, and then we are no more. The event of consciousness is gone even as it appears.

The poetic meditations of Qōhelet in *Ecclesiastes* draws out this continual churning of phenomena in nature. He compares all things to a vapor, barely substantial, and easily dissipated. He proclaims that everything and its opposite has a time; there is a time for dancing and a time for mourning, a time for sowing and a time for reaping. In this, he dignifies each thing as appropriate for its particular moment, but we cannot escape the implication here that the timeliness of phenomena inevitably includes the passing away and un-timeliness of all things. The grass withers and the flower fades. The leaves fall and winter arrives. But the snow melts and the flowers bloom. So on down the ages.

Martin Heidegger spoke of an authentic practice of our insubstantiality and indeterminacy as our "being-towards-death." Daily, we walk side by side with death. We noted before that our being-there provides "the possibility of possibilities," but now we see that death remains for us an inextricable part of our being-there as well. It both constitutes it and provides it with dynamic form. In a dramatic reversal, we come to understand that *the end of possibilities is, paradoxically, the ground of all our possibilities.* To have a set of possibilities includes the possibility that we may come to have no more possibilities — death.

Nishitani Keiji, a Zen Buddhist and a student of Heidegger's, expands his teacher's notion of being-towards-death by describing our encounter with "nihility" as the confrontation with a nothingness which raises the religious question for every person[4]. A multitude of possible events harbor the capacity to throw this nihility in our face — from the death of a loved one to the most mundane disappointment — the point is that in our realization of this nihility our existence becomes a question to ourselves. A doubt seems to slither up from our very foundation, calling everything into question. In fact, Zen informs us that this doubt is the world's doubting of itself. In us, the world comes to be doubted. And why shouldn't it? It is nothing, after all. Vapor such as we are, clinging so tenuously to existence, it would be strange were we not to doubt ourselves.

As a Zen practitioner, Nishitani's philosophy owes a debt to the great Zen teacher Dōgen (1200-1253). We find amongst Dōgen's

---

4. Keiji Nishitani. *Religion and Nothingness.* (Berkeley, CA: University of California Press, 1983), 3-4.

teachings a concept now referred to as *Uji* (□□) — translated "time-being" — which attempts to dislodge his student's attachment to a substantial or permanent being. Instead, we should see that time and being are essentially interrelated and mutually defined, each providing the model for the other.

Time becomes, for Dōgen, an interplay of arriving and not-arriving, which reveals the absolute coincidence of time and being — "Just actualize all time as all being; there is nothing extra."[5] Just like the words of Qōhelet, Dōgen exhorts us, saying, "Thus, to study thoroughly, coming and going, and to study thoroughly, arriving and not-arriving, is the time-being of this moment."[6] In his paradoxical instructions to study the flow of both coming and going, Dōgen gently re-orients us away from our conception of time as some-thing which flies away, as though it is something separate from us or that we might somehow exist independent of it. We are not passive observers of time, although we are often liable to philosophize as though we are. Instead, he wants to awaken us to our always-already being immersed in time, even our creation of it through our activity of living.

Time is not simply the medium through which the essential "me" passes, but rather I am both an arriving and a not-arriving which appears at each moment. He says —

---

5. "Uji: The Time-Being" by Eihei Dogen. Translated by Dan Welch and Kazuaki Tanahashi, from "The Moon in a Dewdrop; writings of Zen Master Dogen." Accessed at: https://thezensite.com/ZenTeachings/Dogen_Teachings/Uji_Welch.htm

6. Ibid.

"Do not think that time merely flies away. Do not see
flying away as the only function of time. If time mere-
ly flies away, you would be separated from time. The
reason you do not clearly understand the time-being
is that you think of time only as passing. In essence, all
things in the entire world are linked with one another
as moments. Because all moments are the time-being,
they are your time-being." [7]

Notice Dōgen's deft movement away from a conception of time as
passing away to the dynamic notion of time as a series of connected
moments which we share together. Each of these moments is com-
pletely full where nothing hinders anything else — "The way the self
arrays itself is the form of the entire world. See each thing in this entire
world as a moment of time."[8]

Dōgen's *Uji* and Heidegger's *Dasein* share such fascinating reso-
nances in this passage. As *Dasein* projects itself into the future, the
present is constituted both by the arriving of the now-absent past and
by the future which is a not-arriving. The future never arrives, for
we only ever live in the present moment, but the future nonetheless
plays an ineliminable role in constituting the presence. The presence
of the not-arriving future shapes the present inexorably. The past as
that-which-arrives is no longer present in the present moment, and
yet, its role in creating the present moment cannot be understated
either. This experience we are trying to outline here is that of expe-
riencing the time-being of a finite creature which constantly becomes.

---

7. Ibid.

8. Ibid.

Dōgen counsels the practitioner that "Vigorously abiding in each moment is the time-being. Do not mistakenly confuse it as nonbeing. Do not forcefully assert it as being."[9] We are liable to both of these mistakes, either to say that something does not exist at all or that it exists in a continuous or permanent state. This second one in particular would seem to be the Western mistake of choice — we elevate the eternal, the pure, and the unchanging. We emphasize the continuity of things as persisting across their moments, dogmatically professing an invisible thread which lends something its essential identity across time.

Instead, against such an eternalism, we must vigorously abide in each moment, for time-being is always-already abiding in the moment. We have simply raised a barrier to this realization for ourselves, and thus all that Dōgen says is needed is to release ourselves back into the flow of our time-being. When we loosen our grasp on things, we can find ourselves again caught up in the play of the becoming processes which make up our time-being as finite creatures.

By way of conclusion

The celebrated poet-monk Saigyo died only eight years before Dōgen was born, but his poetry clearly exhibits a profound comprehension of Dōgen's *Uji*. The next chapter in this text embarks on a comprehensive exploration of Saigyo's life in order to understand how he strove through his faith and his art to respond to the extraordinary circumstances in which he found himself. His poetry wrestles with the themes of finding a home in the continual arriving and not-arriving of

---

9. Ibid.

phenomena in the world. In his wanderings, Saigyo models for us one way to vigorously abide in each moment, and how at each moment our abiding is also intimately bound up with a sojourning.

How does one love the world while nonetheless looking in hope for the arrival of another world? Saigyo's poetry seems to be asking this very question. And this dialectical practice of arriving and not-arriving — is it not also the task to which the Christian is called? Just as God became a time-being to make His home among us, so we must also learn about what it means to immerse ourselves in the world which God loved unto death.

Chapter Two

The Life of Saigyo

Introduction

We're liable to fail in our pursuit of the good life if we are content to remain in the realm of abstraction rather than spending our time in the stories of real people and lived experiences. A human can only live a good life in the location where they find themselves; a good *life* must therefore have a *narrative* arch within a time, place, and community. Each life is unique, and yet each one speaks to everyone else as well.

This may explain why humans have always told stories about the great figures of the past. In these epic myths which we hand down from generation to generation — be they oral, visual, or textual — we offer up the narratives of those individuals who for us represent the profound struggle of each human to discover what it means to live a good life. Their lives issue the challenge to *us* to live the good life by vividly portraying their own grappling with that challenge themselves.

The life of the Japanese poet-monk Saigyo issues just such a challenge to us today. In the life of this 12th century Buddhist monk with a love for writing poetry, we see an illuminating attempt to live the good life, particularly in the face of social upheaval and great uncertainty. In this essay we will explore Saigyo's life so that by witnessing his response to the situation of his times and his struggle to reconcile his love of art with his religious devotion, we might come to see how Saigyo's life and practice provides a model from which we also might learn about living a good life.

'Saigyo' by Kikuchi Yosai

Saigyo in context

Saigyo was born Sato Norikiyo in 1118 AD in the capital city of Kyoto to the Fujiwara clan, a famous warrior family.[1] As a child he served as an attendant to the Tokudaiji household, but eventually came to serve in the "north-facing guard" which was assigned to protect the retired Emperor Toba.[2] This meant that the young Saigyo participated in the court life of Heian Japan, a privilege which afforded him an escape from the life of poverty which most people in Japan were condemned to through cycles of discrimination and scarcity of resources.

However, at the age of 23 (22 by Western reckoning[3]), Saigyo famously rejected the life of the royal court and devoted himself to life as a Buddhist monk. Scholars cannot say with accuracy what his precise motivations were, but his actions were radical and abrupt. Looking back however, we can begin to see those structures which lent plausibility to his actions, particularly the decline of the Heian era court and the contemporary Buddhist consciousness of the arrival of an age of spiritual decline (*mappo*).

During this period in Japan's history, the Imperial court at Kyoto was reaching a nadir of power and prestige. Not only had the court's social and cultural life become increasingly socially ingrown, but the emperor himself had become politically impotent. The emperor's loss of political power can be attributed to a variety of factors, but one

---

1. Bruce Watson, Saigyo: *Poems of a Mountain Home* (New York: Columbia University Press, 1991), 2.

2. Laura Allen. "Images of the Poety Saigyo as Recluse." The Journal of Japanese Studies, 21, no. 1 (Winter, 1995): 69.

3. Watson, 2.

prominent root seems to be lack of revenue.[4] The inability on the part of the Imperial court to effectively extract revenue from the countryside forced the court to increasingly rely on warrior clans for military support, as the court could not support a standing army. The court had not, in fact, had a standing army for generations due to the external and (largely) internal peace that Japan had enjoyed.[5] However, this initially congenial state of affairs developed into a problem when the court was no longer able to control the private landowners. Thus, the only true military powers in Japan during the Heian era were those clans of private individuals who employed warriors-for-hire. Farming operations of all sizes hired private warriors to act as retainers to protect their land and goods, which lead to the rise of an entire class of warriors with no substantial loyalty to the emperor.[6] This meant that large clans such as Saigyo's own Fujiwara clan had large land holdings, blood connections, and standing armies of warriors loyal exclusively to them.

In roughly the 10th century, the Fujiwara clan in particular began to exercise a regency over the land which allowed them *de facto* power while they allowed the emperors to still occupy a ceremonial position. This situation began to change however when Emperor Shirakawa abdicated in 1086 and began a practice which is now known as "cloister government." This meant that the current emperor would

---

4. George Sansom. *A History of Japan to 1334.* (Tokyo: Charles E. Tuttle Company, 1963), 152.

5. Ibid., 150-151.

6. Ibid., 236.

abdicate, set up a suitable heir as reigning emperor, and then exercise his political influence from the safe confines of his cloister.[7]

This political move effectively allowed the emperor to break up the influence of the Fujiwara clan by placing the political influence in the hands of father of the emperor rather than in the hands of the relatives of the empress (usually a daughter of a military clan).[8] Saigyo's role as retainer was for just such a cloistered emperor. Ultimately, this political move precipitated the decline of the Fujiwara's *de facto* regency role and allowed members of the Minamoto clan to infiltrate positions long held by those of the Fujiwara.[9] Thus, it was during Saigyo's lifetime that his own clan's influence was falling off rapidly, creating a vacuum from which a conflict between the Taira and Minamoto clans would arise.[10] Though the Taira were initially the stronger of the two clans, the Minamoto clan won the Gempei War, a decisive war between the Taira and Minamoto beginning in 1180[11] (the year of Saigyo's death). However, the Gempei War had been preceded by extensive conflict both in and around the capital, thus cementing conflict as a perpetual reality during Saigyo's lifetime.[12]

In light of this serious political and social upheaval that was taking place, we can see why Saigyo would have found himself in a state of

---

7. Ibid., 199.

8. Ibid., 201.

9. Ibid., 203-204.

10. Watson, 2.

11. Sansom, 291.

12. Watson, 3.

vertigo. What would become of his clan? What would become of the arts and literature which flourished in the Heian court? What would become of Japanese culture itself? His world was being torn apart by warring clans who were ultimately motivated by nothing more than their own self-interest. Saigyo watched as dark clouds of uncertainty gathered on the horizon of history.

Saigyo's card in the 'Hyakkunin Isshu' (a collection of 100 masterful waka poems)

The Age of *Mappo*

In the midst of this looming cultural devastation, Saigyo could turn to Buddhism for a religious interpretation of these events. Buddhist thought provided a framework for making sense of this time of decline by characterizing the current age as *mappo shiso* (the Last Dharma Age). This age was thought to come as the last of three ages, arriving as the decline of the world's spiritual state, a time when pure doctrine would vanish from the earth and people would no longer be able to hear the truth. The three ages began when the death of the Buddha ushered in the 'True Dharma Age' (*saddharma*) which lasted for five hundred years. Upon the end of this age, there arose the 'Imitation Dharma Age' (*saddharma-prativapava*). This age lasted for another 500 years before the time of *mappo* arrived.[13]

Determining the exact beginning of *mappo* has historically posed a challenge which depends largely on when one dates the death of the Buddha, and whether one accepts different periods of time for the eras. By Chinese reckoning, *mappo* began in the year 552 which was also the exact year that their records claim that Buddhism was first introduced to Japan.[14] Because scholars believe that this account is spurious and politically motivated, they actually date the introduction of Buddhism to Japan to 538.[15] Despite the historical inaccuracy, the shadow of *mappo* cast itself across Japan from the first moment that Buddhism arrived on its shores and it remained a part of the Japanese-Buddhist consciousness. Various Japanese Buddhists dealt with the phenomenon differently. Kukei, an 8th century monk, accepted the theory but countered it by arguing that Japan would be the place where doctrine could live on and that the faith would always be preserved.[16] He accepted the 552 date because he wished to show that

---

13. Michele Marra. "The Development of Mappo Thought in Japan." Japanese Journal of Religious Studies 15, no. 1 (1988): 25.

14. Ibid., 30-31.

15. Robert J. Rhodes "The Beginning of Pure Land Buddhism in Japan: From Its Introduction through the Nara Period." Japanese Religions 31, no. 1 (Jan., 2006): 1-3.

16. Marra, 38 – 39.

Japan would surpass China, which he saw declining in faithfulness, in becoming a stronghold of the faith.[17] Others, like the Hosso School, chose the nearer death date for the Buddha (609 BC instead of 949 BC)[18], thus pushing the arrival of *mappo* back by three hundred years. Genei chose instead to interpret the 'Imitation Dharma Age' as a thousand years instead of five hundred, thus pushing it forward to 1052.[19] Regardless of the various schema, most Buddhists were deeply aware of the coming decline of *mappo,* and though some tried to push it forward into the future, it hung like a pall over Saigyo's time.

This transition into *mappo* brought about a transformation in Buddhism in Japan, and Saigyo's life and practice exhibit this trend. The shift comes with the 11th century monk Genshin who pens the *Ojoyoshu* ('Essentials of Salvation') in which he seeks to preserve the Buddhist faith by prescribing a specific form of practice in light of living in the Last Age. Genshin wrote at a time when Buddhism was transitioning away from being the protector of the nation (thus being tied up heavily with the aristocrats and the royal court) towards being a religion focused on personal salvation.[20] This transition comes through in Genshin's emphasis on the necessity of the individual's desire to be re-born in the Western Paradise of the Amida Buddha. Genshin's form of Buddhism functions as more personal because it asks the individual believer to trust the Amida Buddha's vow to save all things, to rely on the Amida Buddha's virtue to save the believer, and

---

17. Ibid.

18. Ibid., 40.

19. Ibid.

20. Ibid., 49.

for the believer to regularly practice *nenbutsu*, which is the invocation of the name of Amida Buddha.[21] The hope of the believer to be reborn in the Western Paradise hinges on the Amida Buddha's 18th vow, in which he refuses to attain Supreme Enlightenment until he saves all beings.[22] In this way, Genshin offered the Japanese Buddhist a way forward during *mappo*, that is, through the teachings of the Amida Buddha who saves people during the ten thousand years of mappo,[23] and by emphasizing the need to forsake the empty things of this world and to practice *nebutstu*.

When we consider the decline of the Heian era court, together with the Buddhist consciousness of *mappo*, we are able to paint a picture of the circumstances in which Saigyo found himself, and consequently we are better able to grasp the meaning of how he chose to respond to his world by embracing the life that he did. Saigyo clearly occupied a complicated position within the Heian court. He possessed a courtly education and a love for the literary arts. He was also a member of the Fujiwara clan which had exercised military power for centuries, but he would have been grieved by watching his own clan's decline. Due to his love of poetry, Saigyo was also likely disturbed by the degradation and increasing irrelevance of the arts during his lifetime. This irrelevance would only be compounded by the system of cloistered government and the increased violence on the part of the warrior clans.

Saigyo also would have understood *mappo* as a present reality, and as the defining nature of the era in which he lived. This darkness

---

21. Ibid., 46. On various practices and levels of difficulty of nenbutsu, 45-48.

22. Ibid., 46.

23. Ibid., 51.

and spiritual unfaithfulness would have been a powerful interpretative lens for him. Kamo no Chomei, another individual who forsook city life to live in a mountain hut, later gave voice in his *Hojoki* (1212) to this spirit of the age when he says, "On flows the river ceaselessly, nor does its water ever stay the same. The bubbles that float upon its pools now disappear, now form anew, but never endure long. And so it is with people in this world, and with their dwellings."[24] Chomei proceeds to describe the numerous disasters which have befallen the capital city Kyoto even just in his lifetime, taking these terrible misfortunes to be the natural way of things, and as clear evidence of his age's transitory nature. Saigyo expresses these same sentiments in saying, "I think of past times/so swift/in their vanishing/the present soon to follow--/dew on the morning glory."[25] Together these two express the pessimistic zeitgeist that dominated the transition period between the Heian and the Kamakura eras.

---

24. Yoshida Kenko and Kama no Chomei. Translated by Meredith McKinney. *Essays in Idleness and Hojoki*. (London: Penguin Classics, 2014), 46.

25. Watson, 130.

*Painting of the poet-monk
Saigyo, from the Kamakura pe-
riod (roughly 14th c.)*

The path that Saigyo chose bore marked resemblance to the teach-
ings of Genshin. Saigyo devoted himself to the Amida Buddha, prac-
ticing *nenbutsu*, and cultivated a state of detachment from the things
of the world. Significantly, the *kanji* which compose Saigyo's name are
"west" and "journey,"[26] symbolizing his life as a movement towards
that Western Paradise where the Buddha resides and where Saigyo
longed to be re-born. In order to seek rebirth in the Western Paradise,
he renounced his life of power and traded it for the life of a hum-
ble monk who lived in a remote mountain hut. He sought salvation
through living a life of austerity, writing poetry, and placing his mind

26. Ibid., 4.

on the world to come. This was not simply a choice that he would have slid into gradually. Rather, his decision constituted a radical break with his life and his clan. He must have had a moment when he perceived that he could no longer go on living the way that he had been. In this way, we are left with the unmistakable sense that Saigyo actively *strove* to live a good life in the face of his circumstances.

Saigyo, the Aesthete-Recluse

As we seek to learn from Saigyo's life though, we inevitably encounter the reality that we *receive* Saigyo's life, and this means that we always interact with an *interpretation* of his life. This interpretation of Saigyo's life comes down to us in his poetry, folk stories, tapestries, third person accounts of his life, and the reflections of those who through the ages took him as a model for their own lives. The Saigyo who we experience today is a Saigyo who has become larger than life, and thus represents something more than his individual existence. One could say that his life has taken on a life of its own.

Within the Japanese consciousness, both in his own day and up to the present, Saigyo's life served as the blueprint for the character of the "aesthete-recluse" (*suki no tonseisha*).[27] Much like how the image of "the cowboy" evokes a particular trope and occupies a specific space in the consciousness of Americans, the image of the "aesthete-recluse" evokes just such a mythic individual in the consciousness of the Japanese. The aesthete-recluse is more than simply an individual, but rather comes to represent a certain set of ideals, a way of life, and an archetype

---

27. Allen, 66. Allen draws the name of this character and the general sketch of the aesthete-recluse from the work of Mezaki Tokue.

which informs a people's sense of their own identity. Saigyo's life represents the aesthete-recluse way of life in such vivid terms that he became the model for those who later embraced such a lifestyle.[28] This can be seen not only in how biographies and art depict him in this role of a wandering hermit,[29] but also in how his image was later appropriated by figures like Lady Nijo[30] or Matsuo Basho,[31] who both cite Saigyo as their inspiration for embracing such a lifestyle.

Woodblock print of Saigyo by
Isoda Koryusai (1735-1790)

---

28. Ibid., 66-67.

29. Ibid., 66.

30. Ibid., 101.

31. Jack Stoneman. "Why Did Saigyo Become a Monk? An Archeology of the Reception of Saigyo's "Shukke."" Japanese Language and Literature 44, no. 2 (Oct., 2010): 82.

Saigyo's life specifically exhibits three primary features which came to define the figure of the "aesthete-recluse" — (1) renunciation, (2) wandering, and (3) practicing the arts. Renunciation plays the central role in this set of practices because it provides the overarching framework within which the aesthete-recluse's virtues and activity find their meaning. Also, the act of renunciation (or *shukke* — "leave one's house")[32] represents a concrete event where the rupture between the individual and the world occurs. For Saigyo, his act of renunciation was a cutting himself off from his social standing, his position of power, likely a wife and child, the possibility of future advancement, and the trappings of social life. He turned his back on the world in one fell swoop.

In the Buddhist mind, this turning away represents how one lets go of attachments to the world. Because suffering and anxiety flow from the state of attachment to objects (the self being one such object), the path to salvation necessarily involves giving up those attachments we have to self, society, and the world. However, we cannot understand this turning his back on the world as a simple turning away, but rather we must also see it as a turning *towards*. Through his act of renunciation, Saigyo orients his life towards the passing nature of all things and thereby seeks to truly live. Renunciation becomes the outward expression of the inward turning, much like how in Christianity Jesus calls his disciples to reject even father and mother in order that they might follow him. Saigyo expresses this inward orientation in the words "He who casts himself away/has he truly/cast himself away?/the

---

32. Ibid., 70.

real castaway is one/who casts nothing away at all!"[33] To cast oneself away is to truly live.

For Saigyo, the cherry blossom (*sakura hana*) perfectly illustrates the nature of all things as passing away. These subtle and ethereal flowers emerge in all their glory for such a brief time (not more than a week), and then inexorably float to the ground like snow and return to the earth. "When you consider/all in this world/are blossoms that fall/and this body of mine/where will I lay it down?"[34] Saigyo envisions himself as a cherry blossom who must bloom violently for a time, but who also must drift gracefully down and be laid to rest. He wishes to throw himself away just as the cherry blossom throws itself from the branches of the tree. In this throwing away, one lives not only well, but also beautifully.

In the life of the aesthete-recluse, this movement of detachment finds vivid expression in the practice of wandering. This wandering can take the form of a literal wandering through the mountains, or religious pilgrimage, or residing in a remote mountain hut. Saigyo's life exhibits all three of these modes of wandering. The motif of wandering serves to further reveal the influence of later interpretations on how we see Saigyo's life.

Though Saigyo spent most of his time from 1149 to his death in 1180 residing in scattered mountain huts near Mt. Koya, his three major life journeys receive much more emphasis in later interpretations of his life.[35] In a particularly famous biography which was likely completed 40 years after his death (*Saigyo monogatari*), Mt. Koya is

33. Watson, 219.

34. Ibid., 207.

35. Allen, 72.

hardly mentioned.[36] An expansive wall scroll (*emaki*) from the mid 13th century offers a visual interpretation of this biographical work (*Saigyo monogatari emaki*) and this *emaki* places heavy emphasis on Saigyo's wanderings as religious pilgrimage.[37] Japan was replete with shrines at this time. Not only had new shrines been constructed in the Buddhist tradition, but the introduction of Buddhism in the 6th century caused many of the indigenous shrines to become Buddhist shrines through a simple process of assimilation and re-interpretation.

A scroll from the Saigyo monogatari emaki. Learn more at: https://www.britishmuseum.org/collec tion/object/A_1881-1210-0-267

The specific route that the scroll depicts Saigyo taking was a well-known path at the time, the *Kumano Mode*.[38] Those who saw the scroll would understand that this route was one of potent spiritual power, even a way of experiencing the Pure Land on earth.[39] As he traveled this path, Saigyo would stop at each shrine in order to offer prayers to the complex hierarchy of Shinto and Buddhist gods. This practice was vital for attaining rebirth in the Pure Land.[40] Thus, the

---

36. Ibid.

37. Ibid.

38. Ibid., 83

39. Ibid., 90.

40. Ibid.

wandering of the aesthete-recluse took on the significance of being a religious journey whereby one honors the gods and lets go of attachments so that one may be re-born in the Western Paradise.

This intentional separation from human society and seeking more provisional forms of life comes to define the self-understanding of those who come after Saigyo in their pursuit of the ideal of the aesthete-recluse. The previously mentioned *emaki* casts Saigyo in this light by dressing him in plain clothes, the tonsured head of a monk, modest travel gear, and placing him in vast landscapes where he is dwarfed by nature and isolated from human contact.[41]

While we must acknowledge that this depiction of Saigyo is a carefully crafted representation, it nonetheless resonates deeply with what we learn about Saigyo's life from his poetry. The theme of wandering pervades Saigyo's work, such as in his poem,

> Rock-dammed marsh
> in fifth-month rains
> so full of water
> you can't pick your way
> over the stones any longer[42]

or

> With blooms of pampas grass
> for markers
> I push my way along

---

41. Ibid., 66.

42. Ibid., 58.

no trace of the trail
I vaguely remembered[43]

However, unlike the tapestry, Saigyo's poetry seems to focus far more on his experiences of remote mountain huts. Based on its frequency in his work, this actually appears to be his preferred mode of existence. When he lives in the ramshackle shelter in the wilderness, his thoughts wistfully turn to the seemingly mundane phenomena of nature:

In this lodging
that no one visits
where no one comes to call
from the moon in the trees
beams of light come poking in.[44]

However, we must not see this desire for solitude as merely being antisocial. Saigyo's active seeking out of life in the remote mountain hut brings to expression his commitments about the essential impermanence of all things. We can see this in his cultivation of an attitude of not grasping things firmly in the world, such as we find it expressed in this poem where he considers moving on to a new spot,

When I tire of this spot as well
too gloomy to live in
when I drift

---

43. Ibid., 69.

44. Ibid., 151

on my way, pine,
you'll be left alone[45]

Or, consider this poem in which he believes that he vaguely recognizes a place that he once lived —

Could this be it
the spot where I lived
long ago?
Moonlight glitters
in the dew on the mugwort[46]

Elsewhere, he addresses his self-understanding of his own wandering more explicitly:

If I can find
no place fit to live
let me live "no place"
in this hut of sticks
flimsy as the world itself.[47]

His characterization of the world as flimsy, and his desire to live "no place," shows us how Saigyo orients himself *towards* the world, thus his continual wandering actually testifies about how we ought to be in the world in light of this reality.

---

45. Ibid., 185

46. Ibid., 215.

47. Ibid., 216.

Saigyo's labor to reconcile faith and poetry

Up to this point, our discussion of the aesthete-recluse has remained essentially within the confines of how the aesthete-recluse's life flows from a Buddhist way of being in the world. Renunciation and wandering resonate within the Buddhist consciousness because of the detachment and religious devotion that they engender in the practitioner.

However, writing poetry does not seem to fit into this framework, and, indeed even appears counter-productive because of the way that it orients one's attention and desires towards the world. How could this practice of emphatic noticing and impassioned desiring nurture the necessary virtues in a Buddhist practitioner?

This feeling of incongruity is not out of place. Indeed, many Buddhists during Saigyo's life saw the two as incompatible,[48] and even Saigyo himself struggled to reconcile his life of religious devotion with his love for poetry. What arose out of this struggle was a new understanding of how one could be authentically Buddhist *and* authentically Japanese, thus paving the way for the unique vision of the aesthete-recluse as one who expresses their profound sense of homelessness in the world through peculiarly Japanese forms of poetry.

---

48. Ibid., 5.

Saigyo under a cherry tree

The form and its history

However, before we are able to explore Saigyo's poetry and how he grappled with his values through his own work, we'll find it helpful to embark on a brief excursus on the nature and history of *waka* poetry.

Waka is a poetic form in which the poet employs 31 syllables, typically rendered in five lines of 5-7-5-7-7. This structure suits the Japanese language due to its syllabic nature, which does not use a Western alphabet, but rather a mixture of kanji (Chinese characters) and two syllabaries (hiragana and katakana).

Scholars do not have a clear picture of when or how the *waka* form arose in Japan, but this is precisely because the form is so deeply embedded in Japanese history. The oldest known Japanese book *Ko-jiki* (The Record of Ancient Matters) even attributes the origin of the *waka* form to the brother of the sun goddess Amaterasu [49] from whom the ruling Yamato clan is said to have descended. Since the

---

49. Makoto Ueda. *Modern Japanese Tanka*. (New York: Columbia University Press, 1996), x.

Kojiki was completed in 712 AD, the form must have pre-dated the work, but the history nonetheless remains shrouded in the mists of time.[50]

The earliest collection of Japanese poetry, the *Manyoshu* (The Collection of Ten Thousand Leaves), contained 4,500 poems, of which 4,200 are composed in the *waka* form.[51] This collection, which was compiled in the middle 8th century, contained poems written by those from a variety of occupations and walks of life, presenting poems by people from princes to fishermen, and guards to beggars.[52]

However, over the next century, *waka* poetry became the primary form used by the royal court and the upper class, largely due to the literary arts becoming centrally located in the capital Kyoto. Over time, *waka* came to dominate the aesthetic life of the Heian court. Due to the shift of *waka* towards the life of the court, there also arose a shift in the style of *waka* itself. *Waka* during the era when the material for the *Manyoshu* was being composed was treated as a way to express a variety of different types of experiences, and it excelled in its use of simple language to express the beauty of everyday life.

However, the shift from *waka* as a mundane practice to a high literary art form became more evident in the next major collection of poetry, the *Kokinshu*, which was compiled in 905 AD.[53] The *Kokinshu* went on to define the style of *waka* poetry up until the time of Saigyo. The *waka* which was being written in the court had

---

50. Ibid., xi.

51. Ibid., xii.

52. Ibid., xi.

53. Ibid., xiii.

taken on a more refined style which preferred to focus on the poet's subjective reactions to personal or social situations, with a propensity for creatively leaving details unspoken, and also rigorously avoiding words borrowed from China.[54]

Because of the insular and highly circumscribed nature of the world of the Imperial court, over time *waka* became focused on a smaller pool of topics, such as social situations, courtship, and general feelings of ennui. Over time, *waka* became a distinguishing marker of how profoundly out of touch with the real world the Heian imperial court had become, and thus trafficked exclusively in communicating the experiences and aesthetic forms of the socially ingrown world of the palace and its hangers-on.

This was the world that Saigyo had grown up in as he learned the art of *waka* poetry. The Heian court had grown increasingly out of touch with the world outside its walls, seeing the peasants as not much more than filth and a nuisance which distracts one from the art of sitting around all day reciting poetry or participating in the various social functions of being at court.[55]

Kamo no Chomei comments on the old poetry in comparison to the new, saying, "Some of today's poems could be said to achieve a nice turn of phrase here and there, but somehow they just do not

---

54. Watson, 7.

55. The Heian court's contemptuous attitude towards the poor can be found exemplified in such works as Sei Shonagon's *Pillow Book*.

have the old poetry's subtle flavor of feeling that resonates beyond the words."[56]

There seemed to be a growing realization that the poetry of the Heian court was lacking what had made *waka* so beautiful in the first place. What the newer poetry seemed to lack was an emphasis on the mundane doings of common folk and the description of natural objects which resonates so much with the Japanese spirit.

Chomei seems to indicate that this was what he found so enticing about the older poetry, when he says, "The doings of lowly folk, mountain woodsmen and so forth are beguiling when expressed in poetry, and even the terrifying wild boar becomes quite tamed and elegant by the phrase 'where the wild boar lays his head'."[57]

Saigyo's return to the things in the world

Saigyo's poetry represents a marked break with the newer style of the Heian court, and a return to older forms, such as were collected in the *Manyoshu*. Though Saigyo was not alone in this reformation of *waka* (Shunzei and his circle prompted the revolution[58]), he stands today as a giant of the age, and even enjoyed widespread popularity during his lifetime.

This pioneering style took its inspiration from outside the walls of the royal court, and sought instead to introduce a more somber tone

---

56. Chomei, 76.

57. Ibid.

58. Watson, 8.

and a return to descriptions of the phenomena of nature[59] rather than almost exclusively focusing on human subjectivity and social practices in the context of a royal court which was far removed from any type of labor or physical want.

Consider how these two poems express insights which would be inaccessible to someone who exclusively lived their life in the royal palace:

> Fishermen
> by a rocky shore
> winds blowing wildly
> in a boat unmoored --
> such is our condition![60]

> or —

> Woodcutter
> sleeping all alone
> in his pine bough shelter
> the only sound
> his only visitor, the hail.[61]

In these poems Saigyo displays a refreshing ambivalence towards convention, and instead returns to the subject matter which Chomei

---

59. Ibid., 10.

60. Ibid., 137.

61. Ibid., 97.

believes was the life-blood of the early practice of *waka* poetry in Japan.

Saigyo's poetry urges us to pay attention to how each singular event demands to be noticed and known precisely as it is. He displays a child-like wonder in how he focuses on the most mundane things, and yet he also sees these mundane objects as metaphors for the deep mysteries of the world. We do not need to look at things through the lens of a system of spiritual or philosophical preconceptions, but rather patterns of interconnectedness will emerge precisely when we approach each thing as its own singularity.

Earlier, we raised the question of how the act of writing poetry could be compatible with the life of one who seeks to renounce the world. We might phrase the question in the following way which is more specific to Saigyo's Buddhist context, "Is it not the case that poetry causes one to develop new attachments which would prevent one from truly desiring rebirth in the Western Paradise of the Amida Buddha?" If attachments are what cause us suffering, and hold us back from nirvana, does not poetry work against the aims of Buddhism?

Saigyo asks himself these same questions in his work.

> Why should my heart
> still harbor
> passion for cherry flower
> I who thought
> I had put all that behind me?[62]

or

---

62. Ibid., 39.

If I've truly renounced it
I should show how I abhor
this troubled world
for my sake, cloud over
moon of the autumn night![63]

In another poem, he seems to express an ominous misgiving about whether rebirth will make him truly happy, by saying —

Were we sure of seeing
a moon like this
in existences to come
who would be sorry
to leave this life?[64]

He seems uncertain deep down that he will see this moon again in the next life, and this causes doubts to cloud his mind.

He even explicitly acknowledges how attached he has become to certain phenomena, such as when he says,

Gazing at them
I've grown so close
to these blossoms
to part with them when they fall

---

63. Ibid., 208.

64. Ibid., 158.

seems bitter indeed![65]

Nor do we find him expressing such attachment towards nature alone, but also towards his own thoughts,

> I have cast off the world
> but there are thoughts
> I cannot cast away--
> I who have yet
> to part from the capital. [66]

We also see him expressing profound loneliness and desiring companionship —

> If only there were
> someone else
> willing to bear this loneliness
> side by side we'd build our huts
> for winter in a mountain village.[67]

He wants to be lonely together with another person? In another poem, he expresses the bitter anguish of having no one to comfort him,

---

65. Ibid., 45.

66. Ibid., 197.

67. Ibid., 93.

"Why does no one say 'Pitiful'
or come to comfort me?
In the house
where I long for my love
the wind blows over the reeds." [68]

All these poems speak to Saigyo's own wrestling and anguish, yet are these not precisely the things that one seeks to shed through the act of renouncing the world?

It's not clear to me from Saigyo's poems that he ever worked out a satisfying answer to this question. However, I've come to think that the wrestling itself is the point. Saigyo never gave up on poetry, but rather continued to simply see nature and its cycles as the place where he was most in touch with what was beautiful and sacred. His work seems to indicate that he saw nature as the holy site where he participated in the mysteries of the world, rather than in the rituals, shrines, or pilgrimages for which he was later lionized.

He seems content only to gaze upon nature in order to find himself caught up with it in the simple joys of arising and passing away. Saigyo's convictions about the beauty of the world and the value of poetry carried him forward, even as he didn't have all the details ironed out.

One could choose to interpret this as a crude inconsistency or perhaps a stubbornness which exposes a lack of virtue. However, one could also see in Saigyo's dedication to the art of poetry an expression of the noble spirit of one driven by a conviction which they do not fully have the resources to make sense of, but which nonetheless takes

---

68. Ibid., 119.

the lead and carves a new path in the wilderness. To sit with the contradiction, this was Saigyo's power, and perhaps we must develop that capacity as well to live a good life.

More than anything, I believe that Saigyo was overcome by the profoundly paradoxical fixation on the utter uniqueness of each thing and its absolute interconnectedness with everything else. He knew that he was intimately bound up in this process as well, and his poetry attempts to bring this contradiction into words for us to awaken to as well.

Saigyo from the standpoint of Buddhism

Despite Saigyo's pursuit of poetry and his questions about his faith lacking a clear resolution in his own life, those who came after him saw in his life a model for how they could better understand the practice of their own faith. In an important sense, this is a vindication of his efforts.

Saigyo's death played a particularly crucial role in vindicating his life in the eyes of other Buddhists, opening the door to his life's being held up as a good life which one could seek to emulate.[69] In one of his poems, Saigyo describes how he wishes to die, saying, "Let me die in spring/under the blossoming trees/let it be around/that full moon/of Kisaragi month."[70] In this poem, Saigyo is wishing to die on the same day as Shakyamuni Buddha, who died on the 15th day of the second month of the lunar calendar.[71]

---

69. Allen, 70.

70. Watson, 40.

71. Ibid.

Many were amazed when he died on the 16th day of Kisaragi month in 1190, just as he had longed for. This speaks to the power that one's death can have in the interpretation of one's life. A good death may very well vindicate one whose life may have been too advanced for their own time. In this way, death allows us to see someone's life anew. Because it closes the curtain on a life, the narrative of one's life becomes definite and thus can become an object of consideration to others. Until a life is finished, it still remains an open question, both to the one living it and the ones observing it.

Because the nature of Saigyo's death gained the approval of his religious community, his life became open to being re-envisioned, and in this way those who came after him were able to recognize in him a depth of insight that he at the time was not able to see in himself. For instance, in his pivotal article "Saigyo and the Buddhist Value of Nature," William LaFleur holds Saigyo up as one who brought to expression the culminating insights of a long running debate in Buddhism about the nature of Buddha-hood (enlightenment)[72], and thereby forged a new way to understand existence such that he could remain faithful to both his Buddhist and Japanese identities.

This debate about Buddha-hood has its roots in the reflections of early Buddhist thinkers on whether plants can attain Buddha-nature. [73] Although this question may appear akin to asking how many angels dance on the head of a pin, how one answers this question actually serves as a watershed for how one understands the nature of everything else in the world.

---

72. William LaFleur. "Saigyo and the Buddhist Value of Nature. Part 1." History of Religions 13, no. 2 (Nov., 1973): 93-94.

73. LaFleur, 94.

The debate hinges on the question of whether one *attains* Buddha-nature or if one *already is* Buddha-nature.[74] If Buddha-nature is attained through following the example of the Buddha and carefully practicing meditation, this poses serious problems for whether plants may be said to attain Buddha-nature. After all, a plant has no volition or agency, and thus cannot practice the Buddha's teachings.

However, if all things *already are* Buddha-nature, and one must simply *realize* that one *is* Buddha-nature, then it may be the case that plants, rocks, and animals are more in touch with Buddha-nature than humans are. They just *are*. In this way, this debate poses the question of what sort of problem human beings constitute in the community of creatures — are we the weird ones who have forgotten our original centeredness?

The Tendai school and the Shingon school debated this question when Buddhism arrived in Japan, with the Tendai school initially representing the viewpoint of *shikaku* (that one attains Buddha-nature through proper practice) and the Shingon school representing the viewpoint of *hongaku* (that all things simply *are* Buddha-nature)[75] . However, over time, as the Tendai school eventually drifted into the *hongaku* view, this established something of a consensus on the issue within the Japanese Buddhist schools.[76]

LaFleur attributes this drift in large part to the profound respect and care for the religious value of nature in Japan's indigenous reli-

---

74. Ibid., 100.

75. Ibid., 109.

76. Ibid.

gious practice prior to Buddhism's arrival.[77] Because of the syncretistic pressures of the indigenous religions, Buddhism in Japan necessarily had to adapt to this previous commitment of the Japanese people. The presence of this reverence for nature as the site of the activity of the *kami* provides us with a coherent framework for how Saigyo's poetic work successfully integrates the heritage of the Japanese people. We can see how Saigyo's work brings together the primordial commitments of the Japanese people and an established stream of thought within the Buddhist tradition.

As a Japanese man, Saigyo sought to practice and preserve the poetic form which his people had fallen in love with and which had shown itself to harmonize with the structure and cadence of the Japanese language. He was able to take up that profound respect and attention to the passing fragility of nature which his ancestors held so dear. In practicing the ancient art of noticing nature and speaking 31 syllables to express what he had observed, Saigyo encountered the true nature of things which he found subsisting right before his eyes.

The ethereal beauty of falling blossoms. The harsh cold of a mountain hut. The haunting scent of plums wafting from the neighbor's yard.

He does not need to go to the city or pray in a temple to see Buddha-nature; he may simply look at the cherry blossom blooming right in front of his eyes. For him, there need not be anything behind reality which makes it ultimately real. It simply is itself. Nature natures. The world just worlds. He must merely see how things are and accept the beauty of being at one with it. Each thing is wholly unique and yet wholly unified with everything else.

---

77. Ibid., 111.

Can we say that Saigyo lived a good life?

Having offered a comprehensive account of Saigyo's life and convictions, we must turn to ask in earnest whether Saigyo's life may truly be called a good life. After all, I have repeatedly claimed throughout this paper that we should see his life as a good life which teaches us how to live the good life, but we may at this point still be asking ourselves why we should look upon Saigyo's life of renunciation, wandering, and artistic pursuits as good. Could it perhaps rather be the case that Saigyo chose the lesser path by choosing to abandon his family and his responsibilities in order to wander about and write poetry?

In order to understand the significance of Saigyo's actions, we must recall the context of Saigyo's actions. After all, I want to demonstrate not only what Saigyo can teach us about the good life, but also the radically contextual nature of each good life. Therefore, I take this as an opportunity to reiterate that no good life can be interchanged with any other. Each good life is a life lived by a particular individual within a particular context where they must make decisions based on the situations in which they find themselves and use the resources which they have available to themselves. We must maintain this singularity in order to do justice to the unique spirit and the vicissitudes of each life lived by each human. We ought not steal that dignity from them.

For this reason, I want to clarify that the way in which Saigyo's life functions as a model for us is not necessarily that it provides a precise roadmap to be replicated, but that it reveals patterns, motivations, and responses which allow us to see new options and possibilities in times of crisis, perhaps expanding our own vision from where we find ourselves standing in our own lives.

Having said that though, the deep complexities of approaching Saigyo as a Westerner now reveal themselves. For, in saying that Saigyo's life does not function *for us* as an exact roadmap, we inevitably are confronted with the fact that he does *and has* played that role for many Japanese people. His actions and motivations give shape to an entire life which became for the Japanese people a cohesive picture and archetypal figure.

Thus, in the explication of Saigyo's life, we cannot forget that the people of Japan have already for centuries found value in Saigyo's life as one to imitate through using his life as a palimpsest of the various aesthetic values which have shaped the lives of the Japanese people. In order to understand the value of this, we will need to consider the values of the Buddhist religion and Japanese aesthetics. Seeing the plausibility of Saigyo's life forces us to confront the divide in aesthetics between Japan and the West.

To this point in my analysis, aesthetics have played a decisive role in considering how Saigyo's life may be seen as a good life. What then can we learn from Saigyo's initial choice of renunciation and his resulting orientation of detachment throughout the rest of his life? What about his wanderings and his devotion to his literary pursuits? Though each of these elements deserves individual treatment, these values cannot remain in isolation from one another. They all must hang together and in relationship to each other in order for us to see the picture which is painted by Saigyo's life. Saigyo's life primarily brings to expression the Japanese aesthetic and each individual part in relation to the other is necessary to paint this picture in all its hues. Indeed, each individual element must be seen as an expression of that unity of spirit which Saigyo's life embodies.

This serves to illustrate a key difference between the Japan and the West in how they assess an individual's life. The role of the beauty of that life plays a greater role in the Japanese judgment than it does in Western concerns where elements like societal impact, political achievement, or great moral virtue (as conceived within a Christian and, often, Aristotelean framework) carry the upper hand. Instead, on the reckoning of the Japanese, one's life is more akin to a work of art which is judged according to specifically Japanese norms of beauty.

In his *Essays in Idleness* (*Tsurezure*), Yoshida Kenko exhorts the reader to see the unique beauty found in anticipation and absence, and not to consider these inferior to presence and fullness. On the contrary, he believes that "In all things, the beginning and the end are most engaging."[78] He tries to awaken us to the beauty of absence by asking, "Should we look at the spring blossoms only in full flower, or the moon only when cloudless and clear? To long for the moon with the rain before you, or to lie curtained in your room while the spring passes unseen, is yet more poignant and deeply moving."[79] Kenko understands the profound enjoyment which can be found in lack.

Kenko's words relate to our previous discussion of Saigyo's description of life as the falling of cherry blossoms. The anticipation of the blossom holds profound sweetness, even giving one strength to go on, and while the falling of the blossom is bittersweet, it nonetheless produces in one a sense of the way of all things, including one's place in the world. Indeed, the blossom becomes more beautiful in its falling because it is being taken from us, and in its being taken, we see it in all its fullness. We often say that absence makes the heart grow fonder, but would this not be even truer with the thing passing away right

---

78. Kenko, 164

79. Ibid.

before our eyes? We have it ,and yet we do not. In that moment, we see the full glory of its mysterious nature.

In his life, Saigyo seeks to embody this ideal through his praise of those things which are ever changing and passing away. Even his life of wandering testifies to his own detachment from the world and its illusory certainties. Instead, his life is the same as the falling blossom, here today and gone tomorrow. Holding nothing and taking nothing with him, he passes through life like a phantom. Through the clarity of his spiritual vision, he is present in the Pure Land even now, though he is absent from it. Yet, in his absence from the Pure Land, he experiences the Pure Land here and now through the ever turning activity of nature.

In his essay *In Praise of Shadows*, Tanizaki Juni'ichiro challenges us to see the beauty of those things which are perishable, fragile, and shrouded in shadow. Tanizaki devotes this extended essay to reflecting on the peculiarities of Japanese aesthetics, particularly in relation to interior design and everyday objects. He says, "There is no denying, at any rate, that among the elements of elegance in which we take such delight is a measure of the unclean, the unsanitary."[80] He contrasts this with Western aesthetics which values the clean and the pristine, seeking to eradicate spot or blemish. He continues, "Yet, for better or worse, we do love things that bear the marks of grime, soot, and weather, and we love the colors and sheen that call to mind the past that made them."[81]

---

80. Tanizaki, Jun'ichiro. Translated by Thomas J. Harper and Edward G. Seidensticker. In Praise of Shadows. (Stony Creek, CT: Leete's Island Books, 1977), 11

81. Ibid.

Tanizaki continually draws out the contrasts in what the Japanese eye perceives as beautiful as opposed to what the Western eye might find attractive or repulsive. This vein of grime (which testifies to use) and what is truly natural runs deep in the Japanese consciousness, and Saigyo's life displays this sensibility impeccably. Saigyo's radical renunciation leading to his close reliance on the land and his tender noticing of nature's cycles appeals to an aesthetic which values impermanence and looks askance at things which announce too loudly their unnatural nature as fabricated.

In one notable example, Tanizaki praises the beauty of Japanese paper (taken from the Chinese) which absorbs light and glows softly instead of the immaculate white of Western paper which serves to block and reflect the light with a garish intensity.[82] The soft glow of the Japanese paper speaks of the soft beams of the moon and also the ethereal lights of the firefly who dances in the night air.

After reading Tanizaki's meditations on beauty, one is left thinking that Western standards of beauty tend to be reaching beyond this world and seeking to construct something which surpasses that which can be found naturally. On the other hand, Tanizaki commits himself to the idea that, "The quality that we call beauty, however, *must always grow from the realities of life*, and our ancestors, forced to live in dark rooms, presently came to discover beauty in shadows, ultimately to guide shadows towards beauty's ends [emphasis added]."[83]

Saigyo's poetry and wandering nature testify to his love of that which is natural, speaking of that which is past, and which is even now being worn down —

---

82. Ibid., 9-10.

83. Ibid., 18.

Wondering if it's a winter shower
I wake in my bed
and hear them--
the leaves that
couldn't withstand the storm,[84]

or

Cherry petals,
like the tears
of someone who's lonely
showering down
when the wind blows cold.[85]

Notice how Saigyo's attention is drawn to those things which have fallen down or have perished, which is the natural way of things. Saigyo certainly sees his life in much the same way, choosing to live a life fitting of one who does not call the world home, and yet finds his home precisely in his homelessness.

Through Kenko and Tanizaki's reflections on Japanese aesthetics, we can more fully understand that spirit of beauty which animates Saigyo's life and lends it such potency in Japanese eyes. We can also simultaneously awaken to our own Western context which seems to value the concrete achievements or artifacts of a life rather than focusing on the spirit which animated and shaped the individual's life in general. We are perhaps less inclined to be struck by the form of a life

---

84. Watson, 91.

85. Ibid., 156.

as much as we are by the individual episodes which seem to compose that life.

We do not take Saigyo's life to be beautiful primarily for his specific achievements, although his poetry is certainly unrivaled, but rather we marvel at his orientation towards life and the ideals that his life came to embody. Even his artistic achievements must be seen not primarily from the lens of "culturally significant works,' but as the bubbling up and subsequent expression of Saigyo's way of being in the world.

Saigyo paints for us a picture of a beautiful life not primarily so we can see *him*, but that we can see the beauty which shows itself forth *in* him. His poetry functions as one important element of the overall picture of his life, one which demands to be seen as a whole which embodies that which the Japanese aesthetics sees as most beautiful about life and the world in which we live it.

On not-yet knowing how it ends

A final excursus is necessary in order to draw together all the threads of Saigyo's life. We must consider the element of not-yet-knowing which plays such a crucial role in the good life. There is an important sense in which Saigyo could not have known how his life would be received by the Japanese people. Though his poetry was popular during his life-time, and thus he did enjoy notoriety as an artist, the interpretations of Saigyo's life as the aesthete-recluse which would give rise to an entire way of life did not flower until after his death. This reality seems to indicate that central to living a good life is making choices about which one cannot be sure concerning the final result. In short, we cannot know how our life will be received by future generations, and thus we do not know how it will be received.

Bernard Williams discusses this precise moral dilemma in his essay "Moral Luck" in which he considers the question of Paul Gauguin's life — is Gauguin's life only now considered good from our perspective because he succeeded at producing great art? The sacrifices he made by leaving his family behind, living in Tahiti, and enduring years of obscurity and financial insecurity are only retrospectively seen as "sacrifices" rather than "wastes" or "failures" because we in the present take Gauguin's work to be a significant human achievement. If Gauguin had failed in his quest to produce truly great art, all of his preceding life events would have been retroactively transfigured into failures. Thus, until Paul either succeeded or failed, the events which had made up his life to that point remained *essentially indeterminate* as to their value — depending on what he did in the future, their meaning could go either way.

Therefore, the good life seems to require us to have the courage to take steps which are shrouded in mystery, perhaps feeling as though we are being guided by contradictory intuitions. Every decision comes about as the result of a war in our hearts, and rarely is one side's victory utterly complete in its conquest. Living a good life demands the type of courage which hopes in the midst of the blinding fog of conflict.[86] Saigyo's life exhibits this crucial trait where he lives according to what he can see, and it was those who came after who saw the coherence of his life that he could not see.

In this way, Saigyo's life opens the question for us of how one goes about the process of evaluating a good life. Could it be the case that

---

86. Jonathan Lear's book "Radical Hope" offers one such account by examining the life of Plenty Coups, the chief of the Crow tribe at the time when the Crow nation was transitioning to reservation life.

an individual may respond to a calling and, through a great vitality of spirit, choose to lead a life which may not be the path that every individual should have chosen, but which comes to serve as a symbol of something greater?

For instance, we may find reason to accuse Saigyo of wrongdoing because his renunciation involved leaving a wife and child, or we could argue that Saigyo ought to have devoted his life to caring for the poor who were oppressed by the aristocracy. All these options have a legitimacy to them that forcefully seizes us. Remain within the system and care for one's family? Use the system to care for those who are oppressed by the system? Leave the system to witness to a more ultimate reality? Is there a *right* choice or simply right *choices*?

Clearly, if every individual chose to live as Saigyo did, civilization as we know it would cease to exist. Each individual would live on the brink of starvation and the human race would die off because there would be no reproduction. However, this does not demand an outright rejection of Saigyo's choice as illegitimate. It merely testifies to the necessity of having a diversity of human lives. We equally need farmers, kings, fishermen, traders, scribes, and monks. Any analysis of the good life must ask about what this diversity exists for and how finding ourselves already in this complex interplay illuminates our conception of the good life.

By way of conclusion

What role do such mythic people as Saigyo play for us? They are those who make their lives into a symbol for something greater than themselves. This brings us full circle to the question of heroes and myth. Heroes are heroes precisely because their lives tell us something about living life in general; they become the crystallization of an ideal which lies beyond the particularity of human life but which flows through it nonetheless. Though this cannot be everyone's call, the symbolic life of one person can be a testimony to that spirit which runs through our own lives as well.

Saigyo's life preaches about deeper realities precisely because it is so extreme. Its extremity is precisely what allows it to put into sharp relief the passing away nature of this world, its thinness, its fragile beauty, and the power of throwing oneself away. This mysterious realization may equally as well be lived out in the life of a humble fisherman as it could be in the life of a majestic emperor. So, although some have taken Saigyo's life to be a blueprint, his life also preaches the shocking applicability of this animating ideal to every different walk of life too.

One could be profoundly unfaithful to Saigyo's life by throwing away everything and pursuing life in a mountain hut, if such a life were pursued in a spirit of attachment to a certain image which one thinks they ought to aspire to or for which people will praise them. Instead, one could be more faithful to Saigyo's life by laying aside their own ambitions and following in their father's footsteps running the family business. This would mean dedicating oneself to this life with all one's might, but with the understanding of the transient nature of that choice and finding the beauty in the ephemeral nature of being here doing this and tomorrow being gone.

However, this is also not to preclude Saigyo's life providing a roadmap for another person who may find themselves in the same position of needing to pursue a radical project for a specific time or place. The question of fidelity is much deeper than that. To be faithful to Saigyo does not mean to copy him; it means to live how he lived, that is, oriented towards this world as passing away.

Despite the unique and otherwordly ways that I have gone about describing Saigyo and his life, in the end, we must also be struck by the fact that Saigyo was no revolutionary. He was a simple man who was content to watch blossoms fall, gaze at the moon, and write poetry about nature and living alone. Yet, perhaps it was his simple and pure pursuit of those things that he loved that draws us to his story so much. He looked to the past in order to live creatively into the future. He dedicated himself to the ancient art of *waka* poetry, he returned to his people's religious roots through his love of nature, he forged new ways of being a Buddhist, and he did all this in such a way that he became a paragon for those who came after him.

Nonetheless, his life also speaks to how one need not have everything figured out for something beautiful to shine forth. He doesn't appear to have ever stopped struggling with his faith and his poetry, and he also grappled with feelings of loneliness and lost love. Yet, he pushed forward, and it was only in retrospect that the coherence of his life revealed itself. This spirit of bravery, this pursuit of what one loves, this creative fidelity to the past, the heart which never stops wrestling for something greater, these are the things which challenge us in Saigyo's life. These are what make Saigyo's life truly revolutionary.

Though he did not take up arms against the warring clans, nor did he become a vocal social activist, Saigyo's life still lays the seeds of revolution even today. In any age, a person who has been inspired by Saigyo's life will not remain silent, but will preach peace loudly with their words and their deeds. Be that in a mountain hut, a hospital clinic, a microphone, or on a factory floor, we can discover how many ways there are to throw ourselves away in this life.

Chapter Three

Every Sunset is a Moonrise

-1-

Life in utero
Origin at twenty-one
Who is being born?
An idol to these vain thoughts?
A vessel built for service?

***

-2-

Huddled amongst the rocks
Our bodies held together
Ringed about by snow
Clinging to each other for warmth
Though I had never known her

***

-3-

A place I prepared
It sleeps in my bed at night
Long as it slumbers
I shall not have space for her
A thief steals all her kisses

***

-4-

If I believed that
I was unworthy of your love
Falling in darkness
Would you hold me in your arms
And show me that I am wrong?

***

-5-

In one tree I find
More there than I could unearth
A lifetime well spent
Our eyes are not wide enough
For the wonder of this world

***

-6-

Of ovens and stoves
There is more than I had thought
This crushing pressure
So why do I feel this way?
I am ashamed of wonder

***

-7-

Yearning silently
There is more meaning in me
Than one life could hold
Though I choose to move forward
I will mourn what never was

***

-8-

Feet slowly finding
The cold corners of the bed
This morning delight!
Numb toes caress the soft sheets
Soon though, they will grow too warm

***

-9-

The end of a day
But with duties left undone
A felt absence
There is still room for more life
Hours squandered and empty

***

-10-

To love a woman
Forces a man to be someone
I cannot emerge
Please, do not look too closely
You will find my wretchedness

***

-11-

The weight is crushing
If I turned my attention
To each person here
I would be utterly lost
In the flood of fear and joy

***

-12-

Asking for God's plan
I fear what may lie beyond
This fork in the road
Feeble as I am, still though
My steps fall fast before me

***

-13-

Unearthing meaning
The ongoing process of
A man in tension
What do I do with this thing?
For now, put it over there

***

-14-

The hardness of heart
The toxin of the cynic
Flowing through my veins
What I see at work in me
Has infected my brother

***

-15-

The moon is full tonight
Though it is the clouds which move
The moon seems to sail
Floating on smoky oceans
Traveling to the far side

***

-16-

I have watched you too
Why was I not bold enough?
You broke the silence
We stumble shyly through it
But secretly, I am happy

***

-17-

The patch is ugly
Shouldn't we just unravel?
Hour by hour
A garment pulled and undone
Fallen threads resting in ash

***

-18-

Where old meets the new
Splattered and excess fringes
Cracks snaking across
Is it more beautiful now?
Or should they never have met?

***

-19-

Who here sets the pace?
I or the one by my side?
No, we create the pace
Together, flowing river
Both and none, this spring rises

***

-20-

Leaves strewn on the path
Once joyful dancers in light
Now trod under foot
Becoming tomorrow's mulch
We shall be as one, someday

***

-21-

Hiking through the fog
Things familiar are strange
What world am I in?
Life and death are so thin here
Who could I meet in this place?

***

-22-
Trudging through the rain
Fuzzy around the edges
Neither here nor there
The world's gravity tugs me
But I am slow to respond

***

-23-

Coffee drips on paper
The book has been tarnished
As I look again
The stain speaks of this event
Memory and text are one

***

-24-

This lingering taste
Some coffee and bananas
Running from my duties
Living strange worlds on pages
I took this time for myself

***

-25-

There is only dark
With eyes closed or eyes open
There is no difference
Here, all alone with these thoughts
I am floating in this world

***

-26-

Many roads before me
A fire will show the right one
Any path is fine
I will receive yes and no
With open hands like a child

***

-27-

Random encounters
With those who drifted away
On winds we returned
Is this another parting?
Or will we sail together?

***

-28-

The cold is deeper
Early morning chills the bones
A warmth is rising
A cold glass of water for
the body to drink deeply

***

-29-

Listening closely
As my heart preaches to me
I cannot be sure
Are these words dripping honey?
Or God gently nudging me?

***

-30-
Six bodies share warmth
These crags long for the sunrise
Sun piercing the clouds
Bring views of avalanches
Laughter descends on the snow

***

-31-

Everyday routine
The weary unfolding of
A dragging body
But to break that dull routine!
Everything seems made new

***

Chapter Four

Comments on selected poems

I n this section I offer some commentary and interpretations on a few select poems from the collection. I've picked these pieces in an attempt to capture some of the primary themes which run through the collection, but they are by no means exhaustive.

I hope that these brief comments can help you begin to feel how *waka* conveys experiences, as well as the type of mindset which it inculcates in the one who practices it. Perhaps after reading this work you will want to write your own *waka* poems! If that's the case, I will have considered my work a success. May you make the world a more beautiful place by noticing and speaking its wonders.

***

In one tree I find

More there than I could unearth
A lifetime well spent
Our eyes are not wide enough
For the wonder of this world

One theme that ran through my work was the discovery of the effulgence of meaning in the world, and the corresponding privilege that finite life enjoys in the continual excavation of that meaning. I realized that because of my smallness, the world could never be boring. My being who I am and my having only this particular set of possibilities was not something to be lamented, but actually the height of adventure. Everything in the communion of beings promised more possible meaning than could ever be mine.

***

Yearning silently
There is more meaning in me
Than one life could hold
Though I choose to move forward
I will mourn what never was

However, I do not want to pass over in silence those possibilities which I did not choose. Because of our finiteness, we cannot choose every path to be actual for us. We cannot float in the realm of possibilities forever, for, not to act *is* to act. We must choose a path, whether we like it or not, whether we feel prepared for it or not.

In many cases too, there were many legitimate paths open to us. Perhaps indeed many of them were even *good* paths. I could choose to eat pizza, a gyro, or a salad for lunch. Am I wrong in choosing any of them? Perhaps I am, if I am trying to work on my weight, the pizza would be a less than optimal option. But if I am healthy or not paying particular attention to my weight, can anyone bring an accusation against me for choosing any of these three options? But, of course, I had to choose, even if I had decided to eat nothing at all.

Perhaps though we turn our attention to more monumental decisions, like whom to marry, where to work, or where to live. Even in this realm, we are surprised to find that there are many options available to us, many of them good, even very good. Perhaps I could move to Maine and live a quiet life as a fisherman. Perhaps I could decide that I wish to travel and become a citizen of a different nation. Maybe I choose to move back to my hometown, perhaps to care for my parents. Which option is right? One cannot necessarily say from the list alone. All of them hold possibilities, many of them good, though none perfect, and all promise a different way of being that will contain the beauty of living a life.

This poem mourns those good things which could have been but were not. We need not console ourselves by gainsaying the goodness of the other paths which we chose to forego — they are allowed to be good for their own sake, and we can honor them as such. Although they never existed, they lived within us, and in some sense, we will carry them with us as we continue our adventure. Rather than letting them weigh us down, we can mourn their loss, thank them for their goodness, and turn ourselves with resolution to the path laid out before us.

***

Unearthing meaning
The ongoing process of
A man in tension
What do I do with this thing?
For now, put it over there

Nor do I wish to pass over the difficulty of this process of excavation. Indeed, we often feel torn or in tension. This is not a bad thing. The true tragedy would be allowing this tension to paralyze us or lead us to make a cowardly decision. But the feeling of tension means that one has truly immersed themselves in their possibilities such that many of them have gripped one with strong claims. Their adventures are calling loudly. This is the joy of having possibilities!

In this *waka*, I express the sense of being so engrossed in my work that I felt I was unearthing more than I had the resources to make sense of at the time. When many different things are bubbling up, or the meaning seems too effulgent, we can become overstimulated. We must not let this stop us in our tracks. Instead, we must soberly assess what we have discovered by carefully putting it somewhere else for the time being, perhaps returning to it later or not at all. In time, that object's connections may become visible to us in a new way, and suddenly we will discover in it a resource for a new possibility that we hadn't seen before.

***

In *Every Sunset is a Moonrise*, I explore various snapshots of events that I have experienced. The two that I have chosen below involve experiences with people, and the next two I have chosen involve objects found in my environment. These each provide a freeze-frame of one particular event and thus simply one perspective on them.

There is a totality of significance to each of these events which can never be captured in one finite being's experience. In each of these events, a meaning could arise which is either (1) outside of my realm of possibilities, (2) discoverable if I go back in my memory, or (3) not yet possible for me but might be in the future. This is not even to address what possible meaning these events could have for the reader who is situated within a different life and location.

***

Huddled amongst rocks
Our bodies held together
Ringed about by snow
Clinging to each other for warmth
Though I had never known her

Who here sets the pace?
I or the one by my side?
No, we create the pace

Together, flowing river
Both and none, this spring rises

The first poem describes my experience hiking up a snow field on
Mt. Rainier at 2 am. I was with a large party of friends and co-workers,
and we were on a cold and treacherous journey. We finally found a
patch of rocks jutting up from the snowfield, and we found amongst
them solid ground upon which we rested. As I sat there resting, a small
young woman asked me if I would hold her, because the wind was
blowing over us harshly. I knew her name, but I had never spoken
with her before. Yet, I took her in my arms, and we wrapped ourselves
around each other. There, in the dark, I held a person I had never
known, and likely will never see again, but I held her closer and tighter
than maybe any person I had to that point in my life.

This did not strike me as odd at the time. At the time, it made
complete sense. I was thankful to have someone to share warmth with,
and since I knew she was much smaller than me, I was keenly aware of
how cold she must have been. The strength that gave me was great.
Only when I look back on it does it evoke in me a sense of wistfulness,
as though we had together inhabited an entirely liminal space carved
out from existence. Reflecting on it, I feel as if something burned
violently and brightly for a moment, and then disappeared in a flash,
leaving a dark spot in my vision.

The second poem describes my experience hiking the Appalachian
trail with some friends during fall break. I composed this poem in the
moment, as I and a friend were hiking side by side. My ankles were
in pain because I had not brought the proper footwear, so he had
stayed behind with me. As we talked, I soon realized that together our
bodies had fallen into rhythm with each other. The poem expresses
the questions that arose in my mind. It came to feel that neither of

us was leading but simply that we had achieved some sort of unity. A transpersonal flow was rising up to express itself in us. It seems to me that every experience could this sort of thing, if only we would let it. An experience is a relation revealing itself with great intensity. This experience possesses a unity prior to any subject-object relation or discourse. It is the coming to expression of something that includes and exceeds the two terms of the experience. In a way, an experience is an eruption of the infinite into the finite realm.

***

Leaves strewn on the path
Once joyful dancers in light
Now trod under foot
Becoming tomorrow's mulch
We shall all be one, someday

A yellow hydrant
Standing alone in the cold
Watching silently
This sentry observes the night
As people speed through stop signs

These two poems explore more interactions with objects, in the first case more natural, and in the second case urban objects which are constructed but which nonetheless play a role in common human life. The first poem represents something of a mirroring of Saigyo's style, seeing the passing and fragile way of nature as being the shape of one's own life too. We are natural. We arise and pass away. Seeing this same cycle played out before us, and in such noble fashion, represents an exhortation to playing our part well. It also asks about what death might be or what purpose it might serve. In the death of the leaves, we discover that we have a meaning beyond our death and that our lives, even in death, serve to actualize new possibilities for others.

The second poem does not seek as much to draw some conclusion or conscious meditation. Rather, it seeks to describe what I have observed. The hydrant simply caught my attention and that was enough to warrant writing about it. In this case, I drew inspiration from trying to put myself in the hydrant's place. It was a cold night, and I imagined how the hydrant must stand there in the cold all night long. Then, I realized that the hydrant must regularly observe things that others only see occasionally – such as people speeding through the stop sign for the intersection which it was facing (just imagine if fire hydrants could memorize license plate numbers). In noticing the hydrant, I was drawn to it for the possibilities for seeing the world differently that I normally would. Though the person I am now may be negligibly different in substance, practicing the art of noticing and always being conscious of the surplus of meaning in the world shapes one to be the sort of person who can live nobly into the future.

***

Random encounters
With those who drifted away

On winds returned
Is this another parting?
Or will we sail together?

In my poetry, I also ask the question of what it means to be with others. Hermeneutics, the dialogic process, demands a rigorous practice of being-with others in our world, and this process is inherently fraught by misunderstanding and disappointment. When we live into the future, we live into a possibility which is shared, and is thus a future which already primordially belongs to another as well. Journeying with others can be a profound blessing or a grave hardship. This first poem reflects on a particular person who I initially had high hopes for when we met, but we slowly drifted apart as it became clear that we weren't compatible as friends. Now, years later, we have come back together as different people and our friendship shows glimmers of promise which it didn't before. In short, we weren't ready to know each other yet. But now, this poem hopes, maybe we are. A new possibility, an even better possibility, has arisen where I once had great hopes, and had watched them slowly die.

***

The patch is ugly
Shouldn't we just unravel?
Hour by hour
A garment pulled and undone
Fallen threads resting in ash

This second poem asks about forcing possibilities and how one should go about accepting our inevitable passing. One may think of the man having a mid-life crisis and deciding to buy a sports car in order to actualize the possibility of being "cool" and "young" again. This possibility has passed him by, but he has failed to accept this, and so he sadly rehearses the outward motions, looking like a fool. The same could be said of the woman who gets noticeable amounts of botox. She has refused to grow old and stamps her feet in a tantrum against the endless grinding of time. In the end, her disfigured face grows unnatural, and we lament.

I wondered about the nature of the patch. I saw a sidewalk which was patched with new concrete, but it was done sloppily and looked out of place. I wondered if it would almost have been better simply to have let it disintegrate naturally. This seems to be an analogy for how we as humans ought to grow old. If we embrace the possibilities before us, we do not end up anxious or dissatisfied with those things which are no longer possibilities or maybe never were. The key to contentment with finitude is not to fight it in unproductive ways, but to instead discover how infinity breaks forth in our particular finite location. Finitude has a vital and productive spirit to it, but this productive spirit can only produce an actual product rather than a plethora of imagined ones.

***

My sincerest hope is that my poetry and essays have, in some small way, been a blessing to you. I hope it has stimulated you to reconsider what possibilities you might have in your life, or whether you've been fighting to actualize possibilities that simply aren't yours for the taking. We can grow so wrapped up in what we can't have, that we forget to be thankful for what we do have. As long as we draw breath, we have possibilities to be anew. In this, we see our likeness unto God.

As God created creation and continually creates it anew moment by moment, we get to be a part of that process. The Holy Spirit running through everything provides the vital and effulgent Life that wells up unto new possibilities and ways of being. This continual actualization of possibilities is how the finite revels in the boundless infinity of its Creator. It springs up to bring Him glory, but because it is finite and He infinite, this approach to His glory must remain approximate. In this way, the finite reaching to embrace its God results in endless proliferation because this very reaching is God reaching in His creation towards Himself, catching us up in His eternal love and making us party to His adventure.

Glory be unto the Father, the Son, and the Holy Spirit, as it was in the beginning, is now, and ever shall be. Amen.

Afterword

It has been 5 years since I wrote the poetry and essays in this collection, and yet they feel more relevant than ever. So much has changed since then — I've held three jobs, worked many side gigs, I've married a wonderful wife, I have a beautiful son, I have another child on the way, and many many more things besides — but the themes that jump out of this work are still quandaries that I return to daily. The wrestling continues.

To close this book, I'd like to briefly share about what I'm working on right now, in case you might be interested in learning more or getting involved.

In January of 2023, I decided to pursue my dream of building a public body of work. I enrolled in a creator accelerator, I started writing a book I've wanted to write for a long time, and I also publicly committed to posting a written piece every single week. As the year now comes to a close, I can proudly say that I've successfully shared a substantive piece ever week this past year, grown my email list to over 100 subscribers, published this book, produced eight episodes of a podcast, and am very close to publishing my next book *Ideology and Christian Freedom: A theo-political reading of Endo's Silence.*

While I'm planning to adjust my writing cadence this upcoming year, I would encourage you to check out my free email newsletter

Samsara Diagnostics. I share written pieces about topics in religion, philosophy, and psychoanalysis. You can subscribe at https://samsar a.clinic. If you prefer audio or visual content, you can subscribe to my podcast Samsara Audio at https://samsara.substack.com or check out the Samsara Diagnostics YouTube channel.

Thank you for purchasing this book, and especially for taking the time to truly read and engage with it. If you feel lead to support my work, please check out Samsara Diagnostics or Samsara Audio where you can subscribe. Also, if you enjoyed this book, you might also find some value in my upcoming book *Ideology and Christian Freedom* which explores the historical context and philosophical conflicts in Endo Shusaku's novel *Silence*, including their contemporary relevance to subjectivity, emancipatory politics, and a theology of freedom. The book will be released on Amazon in early 2024.

Producing work at Samsara Diagnostics is not my full-time job. I have a full-time job which God has blessed me with — it's not my passion but it feeds my family and gives me the bandwidth to pour myself out on the page each day, and for that I am perpetually grateful. Writing, podcasting, sharing is all a work of love. My sincere hope is that it blesses you in some way. I am casting messages out into the world, unaware of how they will strike others, but I have been the recipient of such messages traveling across space and time to arrive at just the right moment, in a way that neither I nor their author could ever have anticipated.

Thus, I cast without ceasing. And against all odds, my casting has reached you, dear friend. God bless you.